Counting
with Claude

Counting
with Claude

SUBTRACTION MADE EASIER

Paul A. Britt

TATE PUBLISHING
AND ENTERPRISES, LLC

This book is designed to provide accurate and authoritative information with regard to the subject matter covered. This information is given with the understanding that neither the author nor Tate Publishing, LLC is engaged in rendering legal, professional advice. Since the details of your situation are fact dependent, you should additionally seek the services of a competent professional.

The opinions expressed by the author are not necessarily those of Tate Publishing, LLC.

Published by Tate Publishing & Enterprises, LLC
127 E. Trade Center Terrace | Mustang, Oklahoma 73064 USA
1.888.361.9473 | www.tatepublishing.com

Tate Publishing is committed to excellence in the publishing industry. The company reflects the philosophy established by the founders, based on Psalm 68:11,
"The Lord gave the word and great was the company of those who published it."

Book design copyright © 2013 by Tate Publishing, LLC. All rights reserved.
Cover design by Lauro Talibong
Interior design by Jake Muelle
Illustrations design by JZ Sagario

Published in the United States of America

ISBN: 978-1-62295-785-9
1. Study Aids / General
13.02.11

Table of Contents

Foreword

Students that I have seen transitioning from the basic vertical addition algorithm to the vertical subtraction algorithm have a difficult time with recognizing and carrying out the initial regrouping or renaming of the ones place when the minuend is smaller than the subtrahend. A classic misconception is that the student is able to subtract going from the subtrahend to the minuend or up the problem, and the answer is written below the equal line as in the addition problem as before, and the need to regroup is not recognized. Therefore, the answers are constantly wrong and the concept of regrouping is never learned. To correct this misconception and teach students how to recognize the need for regrouping, I have devised a technique for subtraction that eliminates the directionality misconception and makes it easier for students to solve basic and more complex subtraction facts, for those who have difficulty, with a basic counting technique. The numbers never change jobs so the directionality is constant, and with the use of "the Ladder" and simple counting, a student will never miss another subtraction problem again. This technique can also be used for beginning students to reinforce the difference between addition and subtraction and strengthen both concepts. It was written with both of these students in mind.

Counting on the Ladder

Hi, kids! My name is Climbing Claude. I'm going to help you with subtraction through counting. Come on! Let's go! Can you count with me?

1, 2, 3, 4, 5, 6, 7, 8, 9, 10, 11, 12, 13, 14, 15, 16, 17, 18, 19, 20!

Now you try!

1, 2, _, _, _, _, _, _, _, _, _,

_, _, _, _, _, _, _, _, _.

Great!

How about backwards? Let's count down.

20, 19, 18, 17, 16, 15, 14, 13, 12,

11, 10, 9, 8, 7, 6, 5, 4, 3, 2, 1.

Now you do it.

20, 19, _, _, _, _, _, _, _, _,

_, _, _, _, _, _, _, _, _, _.

Great job!

Remember, subtracting is only counting backwards from the minuend, or the first number, in the subtraction problem. When I need help, I use the Ladder. That's why they call me Climbing Claude!

Let me show you what I mean and then you can try some! Let's go!

5
- 2

How many steps do I climb down the ladder?

The problem says, "Five minus two," or, "Five subtract two." This means I climb down the ladder two steps from the minuend, 5. The subtrahend, the second number, tells me how many steps on the ladder. Watch!

$$
\begin{array}{r}
5 \\
- 2 \\
\hline
\end{array}
$$

___ <

___ <

Now because we're subtracting, or climbing down, we count down from 5.

$$
\begin{array}{r}
5 \\
- 2 \\
\hline
\end{array}
$$

_4_ <

_3_ <

So what's my answer? 3! That's right! The number at the bottom of the ladder is my answer. Remember, count down from the first number, the minuend. Let's look again.

$$5$$
$$- 2$$

4 <
3 <

So 5-2=3.

Let's do one together.

$$
\begin{array}{r}
6 \\
-3 \\
\hline
\end{array}
$$

1. How many steps? ___3___

2. Climb down!

$$
\begin{array}{r}
6 \\
-3 \\
\hline
5 < \\
4 < \\
\boxed{3} < \\
\end{array}
$$

3. What's the answer? ___3___

Great job!

Now you try!

$$
\begin{array}{r}
8 \\
-4 \\
\hline
\end{array}
$$

1. How many steps? ___4___ Draw them.

8
- 4

2. Climb down.

3. What's the answer? _____

Great job!

Here are some more for you to try! Remember, the subtrahend tells how many steps to draw below, the equal line, and then we count down from the minuend.

You can do it!

3	4	5	6	7	8
- 1	- 2	- 3	- 4	- 4	- 5
2	2	2	2	3	3

7	6	9	5	8	9
- 5	- 2	- 3	- 3	- 5	- 6
2	4	6			

What do we do when there are two digits in the minuend or a two-digit number is first in the problem?

Like this.

10
- 5
——

Remember, now we have the ones place *and* the tens place. Sometimes, you will have one ladder, sometimes two. Let's look at this one.

1. How many steps down?

That's right! 5!

2. Draw them.

```
  10
-  5
_____

_____

_____

_____

_____

_____
```

3. Climb down!

```
  10
-  5
____9
____8
____7
____6
____5
```

4. What's my answer? _____

Nice job!

Let's do that again. Remember to draw the steps for the ones place first, always using the subtrahend, and watch to see if a ladder is needed in the tens place.

$$
\begin{array}{r}
12 \\
-\ 8 \\
\hline
\end{array}
$$

1. How many steps down? _____

2. Draw them, then *climb down.*

$$
\begin{array}{r}
12 \\
-\ 8 \\
\hline
11 \\
\hline
10 \\
\hline
9 \\
\hline
8 \\
\hline
7 \\
\hline
6 \\
\hline
5 \\
\hline
4 \\
\hline
\end{array}
$$

3. What's the answer? _____

Great job!

Look to see if the number in the ones place of the first number, the minuend, is less or smaller than the number of the subtrahend. If it is, only one ladder is needed when one digit is on the bottom. We use the ten from the tens place for help if it's a 1. These are called your basic facts. When the number in the tens place is greater than one, something different happens. We'll see that later.

1. How many steps? _____

2. Climb down

$$
\begin{array}{ll}
13 & \text{<— small minuend} \\
\underline{-\ 4} & \text{<— large subtrahend} \\
\underline{12} & \\
\underline{11} & \\
\underline{10} & \\
\underline{\ 9} & \\
\end{array}
$$

3. What's the answer? _____

Now you try!

11
- 8
—————

1. How many steps? _____

Do you need the 1 from the tens place to help with the subtraction?

Circle: Yes No

2. Climb down.

11
- 8
—————

3. What's your answer? _____

Good job!

Here's some more. You can do it!

10	11	12
− 3	− 7	− 5

14	13	12
− 8	− 6	− 8

15	16	17
$-\ 8$	$-\ 9$	$-\ 8$

14	13	11
$-\ 7$	$-\ 5$	$-\ 4$

The Tens Place Ladder

What if the first number, the minuend, is larger than the subtrahend? Let's look. Now we use our place value to start in the ones place.

$$\begin{array}{r} 18 \\ -\ 6 \\ \hline \end{array}$$

Here the first number is greater than the second. 8 > 6.

$$\begin{array}{r} 18 \\ -\ 6 \\ \hline \end{array}$$

When this happens, use a ladder for both the ones and tens place. Watch!

This reads, "8 minus 6," or, "8 subtract 6," in the ones place, and, "one minus or subtract zero," in the tens place. Now ask the questions as before.

$$\begin{array}{r} 18 \\ -\ 6 \\ \hline \end{array}$$

1. How many steps?

    - ones place? <u> 6 </u>

    - tens place? <u> 0 </u>

2. Climb down.

    - ones first: 7, 6, 5, 4, 3, 2

    - tens next: say, "1-0." This has no steps.

3. What's the answer? 1 ten, 2 ones—or 12. Twelve! Great job!

Watch! Look again.

17
- 3
―――

1. How many steps?

ones place? _____ tens place? _____

2. Climb down.

ones place: 6, 5, 4   tens place: 1

1 7
- 3
―――
6
5
4

1 4

1 ten, and 4 ones

3. What's the answer? _____

Now you try! Don't forget to use the steps. Find the number of steps from the subtrahend. Climb down from the minuend. Find your answer at the bottom.

14	19	15	18	16	17
- 2	- 7	- 4	- 5	- 3	- 6

13	19	18	15	14	16
- 2	- 5	- 3	- 2	- 3	- 5

Let's try a two-digit by two-digit problem! This means we a have a number in the ones place and the tens place for the minuend and a number in both places of the subtrahend.

For now, the minuend numbers will be greater, or bigger. For example:

        2 7
      - 1 3

Don't worry, do it the same way.

1. How many steps?

    - ones place _____

    - tens place _____

2. Climb down.

    - ones place <u>6</u>, <u>5</u>, <u>4</u>

    - tens place <u>1</u>

        2 7
      - 1 3
      ———
        — —

        —

        —

3. What's the answer? <u>1</u> ten and <u>4</u> ones, or 14! *Great job!*

Let's try another one.

1. How many steps?

$$\begin{array}{r} 3\;4 \\ -\;2\;2 \\ \hline \\ \underline{\quad\;\;\;} \end{array}$$

- ones place _____

- tens place _____

2. Climb down

- ones place <u>3</u>, <u>2</u>

- tens place <u>2</u>, <u>1</u>

3. What's the answer? <u>1</u> ten and <u>2</u> ones, or 12!

Great job!

You try some!

53	68	78
- 12	- 24	- 43

96	84	42
- 54	- 61	- 31

Using the Ladder with Regrouping

What if the ones place in the subtrahend is greater than the ones place of the minuend? Then we need to look to the tens place for help. Some people call this regrouping. Some people call it breaking a ten. This is when we change a ten to ten ones to transfer to the ones place to make sure we can subtract successfully and in the proper direction.

Remember when subtracting, we always start in the ones place, and we climb down the ladder because the number is getting smaller. Look at this problem.

$$\begin{array}{r} 35 \\ -\ 17 \\ \hline \end{array}$$

Look at the ones place. Can you subtract 7 from 5? You can't. Don't subtract 5 from 7, that's not the right direction! What do we do?

Here we're taking a ten from the tens place and adding it to the ones place before any subtraction can be done. Watch what happens!

Step 1. Take a ten from the 3 in the tens place and change it to ten ones to be placed in the ones place, and ladder *down* one step in the tens place above the equal line. This equals 2 tens.

Step 2. Add the ten to the five that stands in the one's place.

The numbers get crossed out because they change in value. The ladder in the ones place goes *up* because this number went up, or increased, from 5 to 15 when the ten was added. The ladder goes down in the tens place because a ten was taken away. Now let's try.

Remember, we can use our ladder.

1. How many steps?

- one's place _____

- ten's place _____

$$
\begin{array}{r}
\underline{15} \\
\cancel{3}\ \cancel{5} \\
\underline{2} \\
-\ 1\ 7 \\
\end{array}
$$

2. Climb down.

— —

—

—

—

—

—

—

3. What's your answer? _____

Let's try again, this is important! Remember to start in the ones place, regroup or break the ten if needed and change the values when regrouping is complete. Most importantly, always subtract the subtrahend from the minuend, or going down the problem, never going up the problem. Look again!

$$
\begin{array}{r}
6\ 1 \\
-\ 2\ 4 \\
\hline
\end{array}
$$

Start in the ones place. Can you subtract 4 from 1? You can't. Let's regroup.

Take a ten from the 6 in the tens place to break into ten ones. Ladder down one in the tens place, because one is gone, and ladder one up in the ones place, like this. Don't forget to cross out the old values after regrouping.

$$
\begin{array}{r}
\underline{11} \\
6\ \ \not{1} \\
\underline{5} \\
-\ 2\ \ 4 \\
\hline
\end{array}
$$

Now follow the steps:

1. How many ladder steps?

- one's place _____

- ten's place _____

2. Climb down.

$$
\begin{array}{r r}
\underline{11} & \\
6\ \not{1} & \\
\underline{5} & \\
-\ 2\ \ 4 & \\
\underline{4}\ \underline{10} & \\
\underline{3}\ \ \underline{9} & \\
\underline{8} & \\
\underline{7} & \\
\end{array}
$$

3. What's your answer? <u>37</u>   Way to go!!

Now you try. I'll give you the first two ladder steps within the problem for regrouping, and you do the rest! Don't forget to cross out the changed numbers! Then like before, follow the *three* steps to the answer.

Regroup and cross out.

1. How many steps?   _____   _____

2. Climb down.

3. Find the answer at the bottom.

$$
\begin{array}{r}
4\ \overline{1} \\
-\ \overline{2}\ 5 \\
\hline
\end{array}
$$

Try these now!

62	53	74	41
- 24	- 15	- 36	- 13

32	85	76	51
-17	- 39	- 28	- 37

```
  63          45          71          32
- 46        - 19        - 53        - 14
```

```
  44          76          81
- 15        - 49        - 26
```

Using the Ladder with Multiple Place Values

Now let's look at a different type of problem. These will have more digits and the possibility of multiple regrouping. Let's look at three digits in the minuend and two digits in the subtrahend.

$$\begin{array}{r} 174 \\ -53 \\ \hline \end{array}$$

This looks like what we did before, only there is a 1 in the hundreds place. Is there regrouping? No. Does this change the subtraction? No! Then do it just as before.

1. How many steps?

Ones _____ Tens _____ Hundreds _____

2. Climb down.

```
    1 7 4
  - 5 3
    1 6 3
      5 2
      4 1
      3
      2
    ─────
    1 2 1
```

3. What's your answer? _

The additional hundreds place only adds another place value to consider below the equal line, and since there was no ladder for it, we just bring down its value as before.

Look at this one.

$$
\begin{array}{r}
171 \\
- 53 \\
\hline
\end{array}
$$

Look familiar? Sure, it does. Here we do the steps as we did before. Start in the ones column. Can we subtract? (1-3) No. Let's regroup. Next, like we did before:

			11
1. Count the steps.	1	7̶	1̶
2. Climb down.		6	
3. Find the answer.	−	5	3
		5	10
		4	9
		3	8
		2	
		1	
	1	1	8

What happened to the hundreds place? It was just brought down because nothing was subtracted from it, and that's why there are no steps either.

One minus zero equals one (1-0=1). See, nothing changes.

Let's try another one.

Do the steps.

Start in the ones place.

$$
\begin{array}{r}
2\ \ 3\ \ 3 \\
-\ \ \ \ 8\ \ 5 \\
\hline
\end{array}
$$

Can we subtract? (3-5) No.

Let's regroup.

$$
\begin{array}{r}
\underline{13} \\
2\ \ \cancel{3}\ \ \cancel{3} \\
\underline{2} \\
-\ \ \ \ 8\ \ 5 \\
\hline
\end{array}
$$

Now look at the tens place.

Can we subtract? (2-8) No.

So what do we do?

Just like before, *we regroup.* Within the problem, ladder up in the tens place when you get help from the hundreds place, and ladder down in the hundreds place when you lose one that was given away. Always remember to cross out your old numbers because they have changed.

$$
\begin{array}{ccc}
 & \underline{12} & \underline{13} \\
\cancel{2} & \cancel{3} & \cancel{3} \\
1 & \cancel{2} & \\
\underline{-\quad 8} & & 5 \\
\end{array}
$$

Now all the regrouping is done and we can count the steps, so:

1. *Count the steps.*
2. *Climb down.*
3. *Find the answer.*

$$
\begin{array}{c c c}
 & \underline{12} & \underline{13} \\
\cancel{2} & \cancel{3} & \cancel{3} \\
1 & \cancel{2} & \\
- & 8 & 5 \\
\end{array}
$$

— —

— —

— —

— —

— —

—

—

—

_____

What did you get? _____

Great job!

Let's try a three-digit by three-digit problem, but remember, nothing changes. Do all the needed steps for regrouping with each place value, starting in the ones place, until all regroupings are complete. Then the subtrahend steps can be put in place for climbing down the ladder.

Let's look at this one.

$$312$$
$$- 145$$

Start with the ones place. *Can we subtract?* (2-5) No.

Let's regroup using the tens place.

Now go to the tens place. *Can we subtract?* (0-4)
No. *Regroup using the hundreds place.*

$$
\begin{array}{ccc}
 & \underline{10} & \underline{12} \\
\cancel{3} & \cancel{1} & \cancel{2} \\
\underline{2} & \cancel{0} & \\
-\ 1 & 4 & 5
\end{array}
$$

Are we done with the regrouping? Yes.

Can we subtract? Yes.

1. Count the steps

How many steps in the ones place? _____

How many steps in the tens place? _____

How many steps in the hundreds place? _____

2. Climb down.

3. Find the answer.

$$\begin{array}{r}
\;\;\underline{10}\;\;\underline{12} \\
3\;\;\not1\;\;\not2 \\
\underline{2}\;\;\not0\;\;\;\; \\
-\;\;1\;\;4\;\;5 \\
\hline
\end{array}$$

— — —

— —

— —

— —

—
_____

What's the answer? _____

Great job!

Now you try some on your own. You can do it!

183   274   322

- 46   - 125   - 146

735	541	612
- 256	- 378	- 476

Final Thoughts

Be sure to

☐ always start your action in the ones place
☐ read the problem and ask yourself if the subtraction is possible. If it is, do it; if not, begin the regrouping process using the tens place
☐ ladder up in the ones place, and ladder down in the tens place, and do the same going left for every regrouping needed.

Any time you get help from the next place value to the left, the ladder where one is added goes up above the place value that is regrouping. The ladder where one is taken from goes down below the number in that place value.

After *all* the regrouping is finished, do the steps that lead to the answer.

1. *Count the steps down using the subtrahend for each place value.*

2. *Climb down from the minuend.*

3. *Find your answer at the bottom when your counting is finished.*

And you're done!